WHO TOLD YOU THAT YOU WERE NAKED?

KAREN L. PRYOR

Xulon Press

Xulon Press
2301 Lucien Way #415
Maitland, FL 32751
407.339.4217
www.xulonpress.com

© 2020 by Karen L Pryor

All rights reserved solely by the author. The author guarantees all contents are original and do not infringe upon the legal rights of any other person or work. No part of this book may be reproduced in any form without the permission of the author. The views expressed in this book are not necessarily those of the publisher.

Unless otherwise indicated, Bible quotations are taken from the from the New International Version of the Bible. Copyright © 1981,1986,1989, and 1992 by Rainbow Studies Inc. Used by permission. All rights reserved.

Verses marked THE MESSAGE are taken from The Message version of the Bible. Copyright © 1993, 1994, 1995, 1996, 2000, 2001, 2002 by NavPress Publishing Group. Used by permission. All rights reserved.

Printed in the United States of America.

ISBN-13: 978-1-5456-6800-9

WHO TOLD YOU THAT YOU WERE NAKED?

This book is dedicated to anyone who has struggled with their identity because of lies that were whispered to them causing them to doubt who they are and who God has created them to be before they breathed their first breath. Be encouraged God is not through with you!

Hold on, help is on the way!

ACKNOWLEDGMENTS

*This is the word that came to Jeremiah from the L*ORD*: "This is what the L*ORD*, the God of Israel, says: 'Write in a book all the words I have spoken to you (Jeremiah 30:1-2)*

*T**hank you God for the words You gave me to write in this book. I did exactly what You told me to do concerning this project and I pray that You are pleased with my offering. I love You with all my heart and soul. Your Servant, Karen.*

WITH SPECIAL THANKS:

To Minister Grant Dufrense of Grant Dufrense Graphics for the beautiful book cover design! Your expertise and careful attention to detail is second to none! I appreciate your ear to hear my heart about what God was saying concerning the cover design. You heard my heart and designed a cover that I believe will cause God's people to be inspired to pick up His book read what He poured out through me on the pages of this book.

Also, I would like to thank my family, friends and prayer partners; who continue to pray for me as I walk out my ministry assignment in this season for such a time as this. Thank you for covering me, sowing seeds, and keeping me lifted up in prayer.

Love you all to life!

CONTENTS

Acknowledgments ix
With Special Thanks: xi
Introduction xv

1. In the Beginning and God Said 1
2. Then God Said. 11
3. The Gardens, the Rivers and the Man 19
4. It's Not Good for Man to Be Alone 27
5. Naked and Not Ashamed. 33
6. And God Commanded 39
7. "Did God Really Say That? Word Wounds". 43
8. "Eyes Wide Open" 49
9. "Adam, Where are you?" 55
10. "Who Told you That You Were Naked?" 59
11. "The Blame Game". 65
12. "Consequences, Consequences, So God Said" 69
13. "The Fall" 79
14. "And the Last Shall be First, The Second Adam" 83

Introduction

In the beginning was the Word, and the Word was with God and the Word was God. He was with God in the beginning. Through Him all things were made, without Him nothing was made that has been made. (John 1:1-3 NIV)

Everything begins with a word. The first word God spoke when creating the earth was "let." The word "let" means to give permission or opportunity to or to allow. God had to give His creation permission to appear from its dormant hiding place. Once God spoke the word "let," then and only then, could anything appear in the earth. In other words, nothing happens until God speaks. This one word "let," or God's "Yes," is the catalyst that caused a reaction to initiate momentum. It is God's "Yes" that should propel us into action to do and be all that He has created us to be In Him.

The same power that God used through His Word, His "yes amen" to create the earth and everything in it is the same power and authority that we have to speak and create. Words are powerful and when used correctly can ignite a fire that reveals God's original purpose for a person's life, but words misused can quench that fire and destroy purpose.

The book "Who Told You That You Were Naked?" looks at creation and how God used the Word to speak and create all that we see and all that we are created to be from the beginning of time. "Who Told You That You Were Naked?" also, looks at how the same words God uses to create and build, the enemy uses to distort and tear down the truth to trick us into forfeiting our Kingdom rights and authority. At some point in our lives, we may experience that "aha" moment when God asks the question, "Who told you that you were naked?" It is at that moment we realize that we are naked because the enemy lied, tricked and then exposed our nakedness. During this "aha" moment we also see that we need God to cover and redeem what the enemy has stolen.

As we turn the pages of this book we will see that God's first children Adam and Eve made mistakes that are similar to our own faults. As we reflect on this, the sovereignty of a loving Father shines forth and how He loves mankind in spite of our flaws and imperfections. God's love for mankind is compassionate, kind and corrective, just as we received correction as children from our parents. God's love also includes provision for our needs and protection from harm and danger. A part of God's protection is shelter from words that cut and mislead His children. As His children this covering stands firm as we listen and obey.

Introduction

Naked we came into this world and naked we will leave when it is time, but we do not need the lies of the enemy to tell us who we are in the dash between the dates when we were born and when we die. God, our heavenly Father, is the One and only One that knows what He has deposited in us while we were still in the waters of our mother's womb. God the master craftsman, the consuming fire can work underwater to create His masterpiece and in His time with one word reveal what He has been working on before the beginning of time. It does not yet appear what God is doing under the surface, but when He is ready all that He is working on will surface for the whole world to see, His Glory fully manifested in us individually and collectively. To God be the Glory!

CHAPTER ONE
IN THE BEGINNING AND GOD SAID

In the beginning God created the heavens and the earth. Now the earth was formless and empty, darkness was over the surface of the deep, and the Spirit of God was hovering over the waters. And God said, "Let there be light," and there was light. (Genesis 1:1-3)

And God said it, and it was! One word from God can change the atmosphere in an instant. One word, a simple yes or no can route an individual's future. God's yes weighs volumes and can be that push, that momentum that can catapult a person into their destiny and purpose. God's no is the loving protection of a father's hand keeping us from hurt, harm or danger. It was God's yes that created everything. It was God's word that caused everything to be that was not, to appear in an instant, to have shape and form. In other words, God took nothing from the void of nothingness. God designed all there was to be created with His word. God used His tangible expression and the essence of who is and is to come to create all that we see. In the beginning was the word and it started there and because God said it; it was.

The earth is God's expression of what He had in His mind, and from His mind unfolded a beautiful masterpiece, a unique creation. The creator in His infinite wisdom decided to speak and what He unpacked from His imagination was heaven and earth and everything in the earth realm. The creation of heaven and earth started because "God said." God, the Ancient of Age, was looking over the formless and empty surface of the deep darkness in suspended animation over the water until he decided to speak the word. When He was ready, He spoke, and He began to paint this beautiful picture that was in His mind.

> *God saw that the light was good and he separated the light from the darkness. God called the light "day" and the darkness he called "night" And there was evening and there was morning the first day (Genesis 1:4-5)*

With skilled precision, God said, "Let there be light" with these words as the backdrop; the canvas appeared, and now God is adding definition. God started with the light because He needed to illuminate the darkness and cause a separation between the two. God spoke the word and then what He spoke was revealed, and then He brought it forth from inside himself. God then viewed what He accomplished and decided that the light was good! God also decided to name the two divisions He created and called the light "day" and the darkness "night," evening and morning. There is always a morning and evening of every day that God created from the beginning of time, and there is an evening and morning in our lives for every day that God has created for us to enjoy and create just like He created. Let us be busy creating every day of our lives so we can declare at the end of the day, "this is good!"

> **And God said, "Let there be a vault between the waters to separate water from water." So God made the vault and separated the water under the vault from the water above it. And it was so. God called the vault "sky." And there was evening, and there was morning—the second day. (Genesis 1:6-8)**

Day two started just like the first day with God speaking, "Let there be" and it was a new day with a new phase to this creation called earth. Phase two of this project God developed a wide continuous area to separate the never-ending body of water, but before He named the vault, God once again looked at what He created with His hands and gave it His stamp of approval. Once God gave His approval, and because it was good to Him, God declared that this "was good" and because it was good "it was so," and in His eyes, the matter was settled. The void, the vault was now called "sky"! God's "so" is the declaration that because I said it, then that settles the matter! God said it, God created it, and God sealed it by His final "so."

God's so is just like the so we heard as children when we questioned our parents about a decision they made. The "why" questions that easily flowed from our mouths were quickly answered with, "because I said so!" The response to the answer was usually followed by a quick agreement not to talk any more about the matter. God's so is the final answer, and our response should be in quick obedience to be still and know that he is God and He knows exactly what He is doing. The conclusion of the matter is, we are His children, and we are redeemed by the blood of the lamb Jesus Christ, and we should be saying in unison and in concert," it is so!" Let the redeemed of the Lord say so!

> *And God said, "Let the water under the sky be gathered to one place, and let dry ground appear." And it was so. (Genesis 1:9)*

> *And there was evening, and there was morning—the third day. (Genesis 1:13)*

Now that the earth has some borders God commanded what he already created to come together in one place so the dry ground could reveal itself from under the water. Again God's "so" appeared because He decided that the dry ground was a required element in his extravagant masterpiece, so He called it forth. He called the dry ground, "land" and finally He named the water, "sea." Once again the master looked at the masterpiece and declared it was good because He saw with his own eyes that it was good.

God does his best work under water. The Grand Canyon, the mountains and all the magnificent rock formations of the earth were created under the water before God let them appear as dry terrain. The glory and the splendor of God's majesty is revealed when we look at the awesomeness of these massive rock formations. God formed these sculptures, and then He announced his work for all to see what He saw and declared good! It is also in water that God created life in the seas and in the womb of a woman.

Then God said, "Let the land produce." Our father God then decided to add some color to the land by cloaking it with vegetation. The vegetation was commanded to produce and reproduce so that the earth's clothing could spread far and wide like a cascading blanket to cover the land with God's glory. God with his hand like a paintbrush covered and colored the canvas called land with majestic artistry. Then He saw it was good and declared it was "so" that the vegetation would spread far and wide, as far and as wide as the eye, His eyes could see.

Wow Day three was a busy day, but to God, this day was, "The day that He had made," and He rejoiced in it because it was good! The land can produce when God speaks to it! The land is productive when God speaks, and even the dry places, must yield to the voice of God. Dry ground to God is fresh ground because He can soften it with the water that is below and around the land, because "Out of his belly shall flow rivers of living water" and out of our bellies shall flow rivers of living water if we allow God to water the dry places in our hearts. There is a well-spring of water, the living word that is hidden within the depths of our souls if we allow God to make it spring forth! Hallelujah! Day three was a spectacular day!

> *And God said, "Let there be lights in the vault of the sky to separate the day from the night, and let them serve as signs to mark sacred times, and days and years, and let them be lights in the vault of the sky to give light on the earth." And it was so. (Genesis 1:14-15)*

> *And God saw that it was good. And there was evening, and there was morning; the fourth day. (Genesis 1:19))*

Day four like the other days started with an announcement from God that He needed more of his creation to appear in the earth realm. God said it, then lights appeared. Where did He want them to appear? In the newly named sky and not only did He want the lights to appear, but when this happened the lights had a purpose! The distinct purpose for the creation and exposure of the light was to establish a way to separate day and night. He also purposed the lights to revolve continuously, so the days turned into months, the months into years, and the years into seasons. God created heavenly clocks to keep time according to his divine will and purpose. The two lights governed the illumination of the sky, and the radiance of each light was enough to light the heaven and the earth below. God was pleased with the lights and the greater light He called the sun and the lesser light he called the moon. And again he was pleased with what he saw, and it was so! Each creation's purpose was different but very necessary. The sun the more radiant and powerful light not only would rise in the morning to dispel the darkness but eventually, it would be responsible for shining rays of light on the vegetation so we can continue to be fruitful on the earth. The moon is the lesser light, but still, it has a significant role because God has purpose in everything, and everything He does; He does it well! The moon or God's nightlight has just enough light to dispel the darkness so the earth and everything in it can rest and cool off and prepare for the next day. Additionally, God decided to hang beautiful balls of fire called stars to assist in the illumination of the night sky. Thank you, God, for day four!

There is nothing more powerful than being in the will and purpose of God and doing what God created us to do. When this happens, we can be the light that God created us to be. Then your natural light will shine forth dispelling the darkness without making a big announcement, "Hey look at me! I am the sun, or I am the moon!" God has a purpose for everything and everybody. The question for us all is what is my purpose and how can I just be the me that you created me to be, so your light can shine through and dispel the dark and bring glory to God at the same time? The creator knows every single detail He framed us with so we must seek God through prayer and in His word and ask God to reveal His purpose for our lives. God will begin to reveal glimpses of what He has been working on and in His time when He is ready, He will reveal His purpose.

Yes, day four God turned the lights on, and by doing so, He exposed and revealed his glory and created a time system that beats at the rhythm of His heart. Only God knows the season and the time He has ordained for our lives so we must tap into his heartbeat to understand when He will reveal his majesty in our lives.

> *And God said, "Let the water teem with living creatures, and let birds fly above the earth across the vault of the sky." (Genesis 1:20)*

> *And God saw that it was good. God blessed them and said, "Be fruitful and increase in number and fill the water in the seas, and let the birds increase on the earth." And there was evening, and there was morning—the fifth day. (Genesis 1:22-23)*

God is thorough and systematic. God has a system and a method that He has in His mind so that everything works together for good. God in His infinite wisdom made sure there was provision for his vision before He created the creatures of the air, land, and sea. He had to make sure the living creatures had a habitat and sustenance to eat before they inhabited the newly created domain. Every day leading up to day five was ordained to establish His name as Jehovah Jireh, our provider. He provided shelter and substance to maintain his creations so they could be fruitful and multiply! Again thank you God for day five! Hallelujah!

> **And God said, "Let the land produce living creatures according to their kinds: the livestock, the creatures that move along the ground, and the wild animals, each according to its kind." And it was so. (Genesis 1:24)**

> **God saw all that he had made, and it was very good. And there was evening, and there was morning—the sixth day. (Genesis 1:31)**

Day six was a very productive day because God started the day off by commanding the land he created to now produce. He caused the land to produce living creatures from the dust of the ground to inhabit and walk around the terrain that was once underwater. Once again a word from God caused the land to bring into existence something that was not there to appear when God said, "Let the land produce"; at his word creatures, livestock and wild animals now came into existence. The animals emerged from the imagination of God's mind on the land that was ready to receive the bounty of inhabitants that suddenly appeared from the fabric of God. Inside him is life and everything associated with life and when He spoke day six He poured out of himself what was already in his DNA.

After God surveyed the land and the new inhabitants of the land God declared it was very good!

When God created the creatures, He gave them the innate ability to reproduce, and He also gave them the insight to use the land to sustain their reproduction. The first part of day six was complete, but God left the best part of day six last, the crescendo of the masterpiece of His work to display the splendor of his glory! God saved the best for last, the icing on the cake, the cherry on top, the "ping" in the sparkle! Part two of day six was to create a living being that was a direct reflection of Himself, "man."

CHAPTER TWO

THEN GOD SAID

Then God said, "Let us make mankind in our image, in our likeness, so that they may rule" (Genesis 1:26)

The second part of day six was quite different than any of the other days. Then God said, "Let us make man in our image in our likeness." Very interesting, because until now there was no indication that there was anyone besides God that was in existence, but clearly the announcement, "let us make a man in our image," indicates that there is more than one being involved in this process. Wait a minute, who is God talking about here? So far, we know God created the heaven and earth and revealed and illuminated everything by shining light in the darkness. He named the light "day" and the dark "night." He named the sky, the sea, the land, the sun and the moon. He even put vegetation on the land and made birds, sea life, creatures to inhabit the land and after all of that God said, "then." The word "them," indicates that is something big is about to happen, something you did not anticipate, something that came out of nowhere.

When God said, "let us," He is saying, "There are others here with Me, others that I have created. They came from Me and are one with Me." This is an announcement, from God, to let us know that there is more to Him than what has been revealed so far. He is saying, "Now, let Me introduce the Me inside of Me, the all in one package that defines all of who I AM. I AM God Creator, I AM God Spirit, and I AM God the Word of life; I AM the Light of the World.

> ***In the beginning was the Word, and the Word was with God, and the Word was God. He was with God in the beginning. (John1:1-2)***

This is "the us" that God was referring to, the triune being that created everything, God in three person's Father, Son, and the Holy Spirit. God's son, Jesus, is the One Who was with God. He is the word that was spoken from the beginning that created all we see. Jesus is the Word of God that came from God. Also, the Holy Spirit, the essence of God, the presence of God hovered over the waters in the beginning when God spoke life and revealed all He had inside himself.

> ***Now the earth was formless and empty darkness was over the surface of the deep,***

and the Spirit of God was hovering over the waters. (Genesis 1:2)

God Almighty the creator the skilled artist that created everything that is and was and is to come! The great I AM that I AM! The one who spoke into the atmosphere and all that was within him came out of him and now had an existence. God pulled man from inside of himself and became a living being because God said it! God created man in the very image of "the us" that has just appeared on the pages of creation. So God said let us make man in our image and in our likeness, so not only do we look like God but God designed us to be like him; we are three in one just like him! God created us with a mind, body, and spirit. When God spoke, all that was in his mind concerning man came forth. God spoke what was to be from the beginning to the end as He saw fit, and when He was finished, God said the word, released it and it was!

Since God gave the man a mind and He created us with a mind to think like him and be creative like him, our words have power! God can download an idea into our spirits by speaking the word. God can release a word, and this word can manifest into a functional object, a song, a sermon, a witty invention, or a book for example. We can speak words of life out of our spirit that God has given us or we can speak death. So choose life!

Not only did God create man in His image, He also gave man authority when He said, "Let them rule over the sea and the birds of the air, over the livestock, over all the earth and over all the creatures that move along the ground." God again said it, and it was established! Wait a minute! We do not want to miss a significant declaration hidden within the verbiage God spoke when He gave man authority, and those words were, "Let them rule." Again, who is God referring to when he lyrically spoke these words? God did not say let "him" rule; God said "them," the plural expression that there is more than just the man assigned to rule over the creatures God gave to be subject to man.

> *So God created mankind in his own image, in the image of God he created them; male and female he created them. God blessed them and said to them, "Be fruitful and increase in number; fill the earth and subdue it. Rule over the fish in the sea and the birds in the sky and over every living creature that moves on the ground." (Genesis 1:27-28)*

So now we see the "them" that God was referring to was a male and a female! So God has given both man and woman the authority to rule over all He commanded from his mouth for them to rule over in creation. He created them as one when He declared let us make man in our image. So the two are one from the beginning, male and female, and that is how God ordained it to be so! These two beings are one and are designed to work together and fulfill the mandate God gave them when He said, "Be fruitful and increase in number, fill the earth and subdue it rule over the fish of the sea and the birds of the air and every living creature that moves on the ground."

God put his stamp of approval on this union. God blessed the covenant between man and woman. He gave them instructions, divine job assignments and an indication why they were created. When God blessed them He did not speak the audible words, "I am blessing you." The blessing from God was an action, and this blessing manifested as a tangible expression of God's gift to humankind to be a living being and also to have the ability to be fruitful and multiply according to His plan.

God's instructions were to be fruitful and increase in number and subdue the land, and He gave them the authority to rule. The increase that God is referring to is not just increasing by producing more human beings but increase in everything that God has deposited within all humans that He has created! Fruitfulness in manifesting all the things that God has placed within us before the foundations of time. God wants us to rule over the land and reproduce more people with the mind to be obedient to Him, his instructions and plans for our lives individually and collectively!

So far God has blessed them, and He decreed and declared for them, " to be," God spoke "be," and now they have a purpose and a being. When God said the word "be" the root word in the Hebrew for "be" is "Cheit-yod-Hei" which means to live. With that being said when God said: "be" He spoke life to them and said live! That was the first blessing because God breathed the breath of life into them so they could live, breathe and have their being in him, through him and for him!

God continued to bless them by decreeing that, "I give you every" this means everything that they needed to sustain them, everything they needed concerning them and everything they needed to sustain their lives! God gave them everything including the breath of life that was in Himself and every form of vegetation needed to nourish their physical bodies. After God declared it, He decreed it, and He established it by saying, "And it is so" to God be the glory!

> ***Thus the heavens and the earth were completed in all their vast array. By the seventh day God had finished the work he had been doing; so on the seventh day, he rested from all his work. Then God blessed the seventh day and made it holy, because on it he rested from all the work of creating that he had done. (Genesis 2:1-3)***

God then took a moment to survey all that He created and declared it was, "very good" and then God rested on the seventh day from all of the work of His masterpiece and all its glorious splendor. God then put his final stamp of approval on all He witnessed with his eyes and blessed the entire masterpiece by blessing and setting apart day seven as, "The is the day that the Lord has made" and He declared it holy. God declared day seven holy, set apart, and He declared this day unique and different from all the other days! This new day is a day of rest and celebration from all the work I started six days ago. I can hear God saying, "This is now the completion of the matter, and I am at peace, and I am enjoying everything that I see, and I am well pleased! Selah.

CHAPTER THREE

THE GARDENS, THE RIVERS AND THE MAN

This is the account of the heavens and earth as they were created, when the Lord God made the earth and the heavens (Genesis 2:4)

A skilled architect does not just start to build without a blueprint, a strategic plan that defines the vision that is within the imagination of the visionary before it manifests in the natural. God, the creator of all that we see, had a plan in mind when He created the heavens and earth. As we travel through the days in God's time that is; the Bible describes the basic blueprint by describing what He spoke into existence each day. Now God is revealing the details that happened as He created the garden, the rivers, and the man. A building before it becomes a structure must have a foundation to support the building. So the first step in the process is to build the support system that will hold up the vision. A support system that will last.

> *Now no shrub had yet appeared on the earth, and no plant had yet sprung up, for the LORD God had not sent rain on the earth, and there was no one to work the ground, but streams came up from the earth and watered the whole surface of the ground. (Genesis 2:5-6)*

So, God, the first architect made the heaven and the earth, and the land that would hold everything that He unfolded from within his spirit in the natural. After the foundation is laid images of what will become walls begin to appear and the building's frame emerges from the pages of the blueprint. Now, the structure isn't just a slab sitting on the ground, but a frame that will develop into walls and you can somewhat see what the project manager had in mind concerning the building. Also on the foundation along with the walls appear plumbing pipes that look like white cylinders. These tubes in the raw form seem to have no function, but without plumbing, there will not be a system for water to flow in the house once the building is complete, so is it imperative that this happens at this point in the development.

As we look at the architect and reflect on God as He created the masterpiece of the heavens and the earth, He did the same thing! He created the earth first, and then God placed streams in the land to water the land since He had not yet released rain to water the surface of the earth. Anything dry must be watered to live, so God created the best plumbing system ever; the streams, rivers, and oceans! The watering system God created had to start from a source, and that source was Him.

> *A river watering the garden flowed from Eden from there it was separated into four headwaters. The name of the first is the Pishon; it winds through the entire land of Havilah, where there is gold. The gold of that land is good; aromatic resin and onyx are also there. The name of the second river is the Gihon; it winds through the entire land of Cush. The name of the third river is the Tigris; it runs along the east side of Ashur. And the fourth river is the Euphrates. (Genesis 2:10-14)*

The word "headwater" means the place where something begins; where it springs into being. God the original head; the one and only head that watered everything that is to be watered created four rivers in and through and around the garden. The first River, the Piston River circled the body of land called Havilah that contained gold aromatic resin or residue and beautiful onyx stones. The wealth and riches of God are ever flowing as resembled by this picture of the Piston River. This river flowed in a circle. A circle has no beginning or end it keeps repeating itself, the beginning is the same as the end, and God controls the flow of the river and the wealth of the river that flowed around the garden! Thank you God for the flow that you sent into the earth and the promises of provision in the flow of your river Piston!

The second river God placed in the garden was named Gihon, this river's purpose was to wind through the entire land of Cush. The word "Gihon" in the Hebrew is bursting forth; gushing! So this river ran around and through the land bursting forth like a gusher of water coming up from the earth, springing up and out like a waterfall! God in his majesty does the same for the people of God because He said, "Out of our bellies shall flow rivers of living water" and sometimes the overwhelming presence of God will break forth from deep within our spirit's; gushing out and the result is we water someone else's dry land!

The last two rivers the River Tigris and Euphrates worked together in unison and in concert, two parallel rivers that bordered the land. These rivers in the Greek are described as great rivers that ran alongside a body of land. The revelation God gave me concerning these two rivers is because they boarded the same body of land they worked together to water land. The same way these rivers work together is how the body of Christ should work together to water the land of the hearts of the people God has created.

> ***The LORD God took the man and put him in the Garden of Eden to work it and take care of it. And the LORD God commanded the man, "You are free to eat from any tree in***

the garden; but you must not eat from the tree of the knowledge of good and evil, for when you eat from it, you will certainly die." **(Genesis 2:15-17)**

As the earth and the streams appeared God added the frame of the structure, the shrubs, the trees, and plant life. Along with all the other trees, God placed two unique trees in the middle of the garden, "The Tree of Life" and "The Tree of Knowledge of Good and Evil." These two trees were set apart from the other trees in the garden. These trees were to be revered and respected. The fruit they produced were set apart as holy unto God.

God's garden was cloaked with beautiful expressions of color. The earth now had definition and beauty to his creation. The land now had hues of green, yellow, orange, and red. God developed the most spectacular, stunningly beautiful and peaceful place. I can only imagine that there might have been some colors that are indescribable that God created in the structure and the landscape of the garden called, Eden. The Hebrew root word for Eden is "garden of God" in the Arabic the root word for Eden is fruitful and well-watered. So the Garden of Eden is God's well-watered fruitful garden! Hallelujah!

God's garden has a wellspring of water that comes from within the deep places within his spirit. A wellspring of water that refreshes the land and produces enough water to replenish the vegetation He placed in his beautiful garden. God is just like that in our lives. Sometimes when we are dry and empty and feeling defeated, God will send a spring of water into our spirit to water the parched places in our souls. A refreshing deep within your spirit that only God can water! A refreshing that no man can water! The water God sends produces fruit, vegetation, and life! Glory to God!

God still had to develop the structure first before He created man, the overseer of the land, the garden. God in his great majesty said, "Let us create man in our image." and from the dust of the ground He created the clay structure of man. God formed man with the clay He took from the earth, and He looked at it and then after He saw that the clay form of the man looked good, he took his breath and breathed the breath of life into the man. After this the man breathed his first breath, he inhaled, and he exhaled, and it was good! Then God said "be," and man was now a living creature. God was saying live when the word "be" was released from his mouth! So man breathed his first breathe and opened his eyes to witness the view and splendor of the Garden of Eden. All the trees, the vegetation, the animals, the slithering things and the things flying in the air! These creatures were just things at that point to man because it had not been revealed to man what these things were yet.

God then blessed the man when he breathed life into him and gave him instructions as the project manager of this spectacular project in the earth realm, the Garden of Eden. God's blessing is provision for everything we need. The land needed the man, and the man needed the land. God created the earth first and placed the man in the garden to work and to keep the

The Gardens, the Rivers and the Man

ground. So God took the man from within himself and placed him on assignment to take care of His creation.

When God placed man in the garden the first directive God gave him was for man to obey him by not eating from the fruit of the tree of knowledge and the tree of good and evil, but everything else in the land; the man could eat. God warned the man that to eat of these forbidden trees would be death. God then gave the man authority over everything He created, and He also gave him the assignment to name all the creatures that He created to inhabit the land. These instructions all seemed like a perfect situation for Adam, and it was, then God decided this looks good, but it is not good for man to be alone, so at that point, God said, "I will make a helper suitable for him. "

As I marvel over all God did in seven days and look at the account of creation, and once God revealed the description of all the details, I noticed a shift occurred in His verbiage, God is now referring to Himself as "Lord God." He is God and the Lord over all life and everything He created with his hands. In this revelation, I can't help but reflect on how the Lord God pulled out of himself all that our eyes now see. As I reviewed the details of this scripture, the Lord revealed that his name "Lord God" was reflected ten times in the second chapter of Genesis. The number ten means, "Perfection of, divine order, completeness, nothing lacking, everything in proper order and a start of a whole new order." Hallelujah! God is perfect in all that He does, and when He is done and completes a thing, it is good! Nothing missing and nothing lacking! Hallelujah!

CHAPTER FOUR

It's Not Good for Man to Be Alone

The Lord God said, "It is not good for man to be alone, I will make a helper suitable for him." (Genesis 2:18)

The Lord God is God. He is the Lord God Almighty because he has all power and authority in his hand. He can make adjustments as He sees fit. The creator has the right as the Lord over all that He created to stand back and look at his creation and say, "Humm I think I need to tweak this to make it fit my imagination and thought of what I had in mind for my creation." So God stood back after He created man and declared it is not good for the man that He created to be alone to attend to the garden, so God decided to create a helper suitable to assist with the maintenance of His garden.

> *So the man gave names to all the livestock, the birds in the sky and all the wild animals. But for Adam, no suitable helper was found. So the LORD God caused the man to fall into a deep sleep; and while he was sleeping, he took one of the man's ribs and then closed up the place with flesh. Then the LORD God made a woman from the rib he had taken out of the man, and he brought her to the man. (Genesis 2:20 – 22)*

God also at this point revealed the name of the man He created, God announced his name when He said, "But for Adam, no suitable helper was found." The Hebrew name for man is Adam, so moving forward the man is now Adam after God placed him in the garden. When God surveyed his creation, God decided that the first man, Adam, needed someone to help him work the ground He created. So God caused Adam to go into a deep sleep so He could pull out of Adam what was needed to create a helper that was suited for him. A helper that resembled him but different, a helper that was a part of Adam, a helper that was of Adam's DNA make up.

Sometimes God will put us into a deep sleep to pull out of us what He has placed deep within us. Things in us we had no idea where lying dormant within us. God, the masterful surgeon, allowed Adam to sleep while He did surgery on Adam and removed a rib from his rib cage to create woman, to create his woman, Eve. Adam had no idea that woman was within him, but God knew it, so when God was ready, He pulled one rib from the man to create woman and when He was finished God brought the woman to Adam.

I can only imagine Adam's response when he woke up and saw God's latest creation. In my heavenly imagination, Adam may have said, "Wo!man!" I wonder if he was thinking, "was all this inside me?" You mean you put me to sleep, and when I woke up, you gave me this beautiful creature, Eve. So, God, you took a rib from my side and from that you gave me a rib to work alongside me to manage this land! What an amazing, thoughtful, magnificent creator you are to be mindful of me to this level that you would to do this for me!

The same God, Adam's God, is our God and because of his indescribable love for us, He has deposited gifts inside us that are yet to be revealed. God knows what He put in each one of us and in time, his time; God will allow us to slumber while He pulls out of us the gifting's He wants us to use to work his land. God will then bring it to us and display what He was working on deep within us all along, and all we will be able to say is, "Wo!" You mean all of that was a part of me, and I did not know it or was even aware that I had the capacity in me to reproduce anything that looks like this!

> **The man said, "This is now bone of my bones and flesh of my flesh; she shall be called 'woman,' for she was taken out of man." (Genesis 2:23)**

And now the man speaks for the first time, yes he named the creatures in the land, but this is the first mention of the man speaking. The man Adam declared what God pulled out of him was a part of himself; she was made from his bone and his flesh, and then he named her as he named everything else and God was an agreement with Adam.

It is a blessing for us agree with God! We want God's yes his approval on all that we do for him. God will give us witty inventions and ideas that are to be named and used to develop the land that He has created! Glory! As we go forth in God in our assignments, our mandates from God make sure God continues in our plans. Until God speaks, we have nothing to say we must wait for his time before we utter a word, because God knows the plans and we only have ideas.

> **For I know the plans I have for you," declares the LORD, "plans to prosper you and not to harm you, plans to give you hope and a future. (Jeremiah 29:11)**

For God knows from the beginning to the end the plan and how He wants the end product to look, but he does give us a measure of liberty to be creative. He created us to be uniquely individual and creative, but we must stay in constant communication with the creator to make sure our ideas lineup with his plan, his yes, and his Amen.

So, yes Adam was given the authority to name everything in the garden including his rib, Eve and then God said yes Adam this is good! God's yes is vitally important when a man chooses the wife that God has ordained for his life because the connection that God is making is for kingdom building. God's kingdom couple must walk together in agreement and the assignment of God so they can be fruitful and multiply.

> *For this reason, a man will leave his father and mother and be united to his wife, and they will become one flesh. (Genesis 2:24)*

There is power in agreement there is power in unity, and there is power in two that have become one. God in his infinite wisdom took the bone, the rib from Adam and created a wife, a helper to assist him with the assignment on the earth. Adam was powerful on his own because God gave him the authority, but the power they received as they came into agreement one-on-one with each other and with God made them a powerful three-fold cord. Adam's connection with the woman changed when God joined them in marriage she was no longer just a "woman" her name was Eve but after she was married her "being," who God created her to be changed from woman to wife.

There is power and authority in the oneness of God; the one triune God is a force that cannot be broken. God in three person's Father, Son, and Holy Spirit, the power of one nothing or anyone, can stand against the trinity of God. This principle is the same for Adam and Eve; they were already one when God pulled Eve out of Adam. In the same way, God pulled Adam out of himself and created man; the original intent and fiber of who he is came from God and apart from God Adam is lost.

Just like Adam and Eve apart from God, we are nothing. We are one with Him, and our authority and power comes from God and God alone. So, we must go back to the original creator and ask Him who am I in you, through you, and what is the picture you had in your mind when you pulled me out of you? God I need to know this so I can be one with you. Lord, I want to walk at your rhythm, speed, and tempo so I can reach the destination you have in mind for me to arrive at the time you have in mind for your purpose and your glory. Additionally, my heart must be in perfect synchronization with your heart so I can hear you and understand the essence of who you are and know what breaks your heart and the things that make your heart glad. Once we reach this place in the spirit; God's rhythm and pace it is not difficult to keep up with it; it is natural and the flow is natural.

Just like with Adam it is not good for man to be alone. It is not good for us to be alone we must connect with the "One" who sacrificed his rib so that we can be one with the Father. God loves us so much that He gave his Son, Jesus and pulled the bride; the wife, "us" out of him so that we could be one with God. We must ask God our heavenly father to show us the place where we fit in him so Adam is not missing his rib so we can be one cohesive body; full of purpose and authority. Once we connect we are one with Jesus and then, we are automatically one with God and able to show others how to find their place in God where they can walk in love freedom and liberty!

CHAPTER FIVE
Naked and Not Ashamed

The man and his wife were both naked and they felt no shame. (Genesis 2:25)

One man, one woman and God all in the garden together. Things were beautiful and peaceful. Adam and Eve in the Garden of Eden surrounded by the brilliant artistry of God's handiwork. The green fields were cascading over the ground with hues of color from the flowers and vegetation covering the once barren earth. There were fresh streams of water in the rivers that boarded the paradise of their home. The animals and reptiles all in one accord and in harmony with each other walking in and about the garden in all of its majestic glory. Adam had completed his work, his assignment for the day God gave him, and now he and his new bride are relaxing in the garden. They were naked, and they felt no shame in the clothes God had given them, their skin. They were comfortable in their own skin because God said it and it was so!

The clothes God gave them fit them and they were at peace with themselves and with each other. They were not sitting back trying to figure out if these clothes fit right, or saying, "How do I look?" "Are my close too tight, do I look fat?" No! They were fine because God gave them the skin to cover their flesh and everything he does is perfect, so it was automatically a fit. Everything fit! Everything in the garden fit, the vegetation, the animals, the reptiles, the man and the woman. God's work was done in creation because He declared it was very good on the seventh day. So God's work was done, and then he rested.

> *Thus the heavens and the earth were completed, and all their hosts. By the seventh day God completed His work which He had done, and He rested on the seventh day from all His work which He had done. (Genesis 2:1-2)*

The world's definition of naked is to be uncovered without clothes on to protect our bodies from the element and the seasons. Without clothes, our physical bodies are vulnerable and exposed to cold, heat, rain, snow and insects. All these things over time can be detrimental in one way or another to our bodies, and eventually, without proper covering, our bodies will break down from exposure to things our bodies are not conditioned to withstand.

With this in mind, God knew they were naked, but it had not been revealed to Adam and Eve that they were naked. He placed them in the garden in their skin clothes and nothing in the elements in the garden was a threat to the covering that God provided for them. They were exposed to the weather, but they were covered by God's grace, so they were not cold, they were not hot, nor did rain or snow cause an issue because at this point no precipitation fell from the sky because God caused all the water to well up from the ground. I can't help but think that was intentional. There was no need for umbrellas, coats, shoes, clothes; God's design was perfect and needed no modifications.

They were naked and felt no shame; they felt no shame because they were in the purest form. Adam and the woman were in the presence of God, and they were just being whom God created them to be and in his likeness. They were the human expression of God himself they were human beings. They were operating as God created them to be and that was free. Free to be the male and female expression of God without opinions from anyone. They felt no shame because at this point they had no sin conciseness. Just like a newborn baby comes into the world naked, pure and dependent. The baby is unaware of the fact that they are naked and they are not concerned about the fact that they are uncovered. They know that they are hungry, thirsty and cold! A baby's response to being taken from the warmth of the womb is, I feel uncovered. mama, I need you to cover me, hold me, and comfort me until I feel better. Our natural response is to cover, protect, feed and nurture the infant until they have stopped crying and resting. They feel the most comfort when they are dry, full and swaddled in a soft blanket. Not just swaddled but held and nurtured by their mother and laying on her breasts and hearing her heartbeat and the rhythm of her heart.

In the same way, our Father El Shaddai, Almighty God, the many breasted one holds us close and comforts us in our nakedness and covers us when we feel exposed. He knows exactly what we need to nurture us and bring us into his rest upon his chest and comforted by the rhythm of his heartbeat. He knows our flaws in our naked places that we do not want anyone to see. He covers the imperfections and shows us through his love and loving kindness that I've got you covered, but you must stay close to me and not listen to the lies of the enemy. Stay in my place and space and I the great I AM that I AM will never leave you nor forsake you, just stay close!

When we are close to him, we know the steps we need to make because we can hear his heart and we can walk in perfect synchronization and harmony. Just like the cadence of a drumbeat, we are in step and in line with our Father, and He is there every step of the way saying, "Left, right, left, right, attention!" God in his infinite wisdom knows each step and each misstep we may make, but because He loves us so much, He will lead guide and direct us along the way if we listen and take heed and receive the gentle guidance of the Holy Spirit.

There is no need for us to be ashamed of our nakedness if we stay close to the Father. It is when we stray away from His covering we expose ourselves to the elements and cares of life that cause us danger and harm. If we listen to and step to the beat of the evil one and evil influences our steps begin to look like a puppet on a string instead of the skilled precision of the drum major walking to the heartbeat and rhythm of God. So, let's stay close to our heavenly Father, our Creator who knows what He deposited in us when He designed "the skin we are in" from the beginning.

CHAPTER SIX

And God Commanded

And the Lord God commanded the man, "You are free to eat from any tree in the garden, but you must not eat from the tree of the knowledge of good and evil, for when you eat of it you will surely die." (Genesis 2:16-17)

Listen and obey; these were the words I heard over and over as a child from my parents and my elders. There were many times my parents or elders would give me instructions with the conditional outcome based upon my willingness to operate in obedience. I remember once my mother told my siblings and I that we could not go outside until she came back from the store. She promised us a reward of snacks if we cleaned up and behaved ourselves while she was gone. In that day and time children stayed at home as long as there was at least one child that was a responsible age and had some level of responsibility. The responsible person in the house was our brother, so he was given the directive, and we were all to follow suit based on the fact that he was the person left in charge. We all agreed nodding our heads, and our brother the responsible one said, "Okay Mama."

Well as soon as Mama left the responsible one went outside and we followed behind him. We stayed close by and made sure we had a lookout person to let the others know that Mama was on the way back. We were close enough to get back in time, so it appeared we were the perfect little obedient children. This plan may have worked, but one of our sisters decided it was a good idea to climb the tree and then jump from the tree to the roof of the house. We were all playing and oblivious to the danger she put herself in, but we all continued doing our own thing including the responsible one. Not long after this, the lookout person says, "Mama's is coming!" So we all scurried inside the house, but it was a little late for our sister the "roof climber" because she was visible on the roof even though she thought, "Maybe if I lie down Mama won't see me?" Really!! Of course, Mama saw her on the roof of the house, and by the time my sister was coming down the tree Mama was in the backyard, and she was not happy at all!

This day is embedded in the historical journals of our family because we all got a whooping that day including the responsible one because he was the one that Mama gave the original directive. Not only were we outside we did not clean up and our sister could have been injured or killed, but God! No snacks were distributed that day just sore bottoms. Before the spankings began Mama lined us up and asked us all individually and collectively, what did I tell you to do before I left? We all with a tremble in our voices in concert and in unison repeated the directives Mama gave us, and that was to stay inside and clean up before she came back from the store. She then turned to the responsible one, our brother and said, "I put you in charge because you were to set the example for your sisters!" My brother with his head held down feeling the weight of his irresponsibly could only respond with, "Yes Mama." Well as the spankings began the spankings did not come without a conversation, a dialog with each swing of the belt, "Didn't I tell you not to go outside? The next time you will think about this spanking before you disobey me again!"

Like Adam and Eve, we did not die physically that day, but our bottoms felt the pain of disobedience, and the tears were flowing freely as one by one we received our lot for our disobedience. Our brother, just like Adam the responsible one was given a directive with instructions and benefits. However our brother was not given the consequence of disobedience directly like Adam, but there was an underlying understanding that the result of disobedience was a punishment of some sort depending upon the severity of the act of rebellion. In this situation, the punishment was severe because we could have lost a sister that day because she was in danger and was unaware of the level of danger she was in because of childlike ignorance.

God gave Adam the instruction and charge that He could eat of any tree in the garden except two trees with the consequence of, "If you do you will surely die." Adam understood God because God gave him the ability to understand and free will to do what was right or wrong. Adam's responsibility was to name everything in the garden and to work that was before him and stay away from those two trees. God gave Adam clear instructions concerning the two trees, and that was, "You must not eat." This instruction is as clear as a bell, you can hear it, and you can see it. God said no! Also with the "no," God made it clear that there were consequences associated with disobedience and that was death.

Although it was not Adam that initiated the rebellion, he did not do anything to stop it and take charge of the situation as the responsible one. As a matter of fact, he joined in and participated knowing that God said, "no." Adam the man, the man in charge of the garden suffered from a case of temporary amnesia and because he could not remember or maybe because he just wanted what he wanted at that moment decided to walk his way and not God's way. Adam decided that just one bite of the forbidden fruit was worth questioning, "Did God say that?"

Wow, it was a tree in the Garden of Eden that Eve chose to eat the fruit of disobedience, and it was also a tree in our backyard our sister was determined to climb as an act of disobedience. In both cases, the responsible one's Adam and my brother stood close by but not close enough to step in and take charge of the adverse situations that would eventually result in painful and regretful consequences. So, listening and obeying walk hand-in-hand together and hearing and receiving in our hearts is imperative in our decisions to obey or disobey.

CHAPTER SEVEN

"DID GOD REALLY SAY THAT? WORD WOUNDS"

Now the serpent was more crafty than any of the wild animals the Lord God had made. He said to the woman, "Did God really say, you must not eat from any tree in the garden? (Genesis 3:1)

The words, "What did I say" forever rang in my ears as a child and the same words I have repeated to my children about directives given concerning instructions. This comment is usually followed by a laundry list of instructions that should have been followed concerning chores or helpful information to keep harm or harmful things at bay. It was usually after blatant disobedience that I would hear this comment, "What did I say?" This question was always before the wrath of punishment was administered, and wisdom was applied to my limited understanding to adjust my thinking. As I would sit and reflect on my willing disobedience and with a sore bottom as a reminder of disobedience the conclusion of my thinking was if only if I had obeyed what I heard, I would not be in this predicament. The predicament being my bottom would not be sore, and other punishments or restriction of things I enjoyed would not be taken from me. The question I asked myself afterward was, "Was the disobedience worth the punishment?" The answer after much reflection was always, no!

The problem with this entire scenario was before the actual punishment my parents would ask me, "What did I say?" and the majority of the time I could repeat verbatim what they said. The issue is I made a conscious choice to disobey and do it my way. I did it my way and not their way. There would not have been an issue if only I did it the way I heard and responded to the instructions accordingly. There is nothing new under the sun this problem of selective hearing and disobedience has been going on since the beginning of time.

In the beginning was God and in the beginning, His children heard him and made very conscious decisions to disobey him. I guess the question of the year, the decade and from eternity past is why do we do this? Why do we intentionally disobey God, our parents, and authority figures? Well, I am stepping out and saying and submitting for your consideration did we get it from the first man and the first woman, Adam and Eve? Did they start a perpetual cycle that has not been broken yet because they listened to the crafty twisted lies of the serpent? Let's look at the first lie, the first act of disobedience and all the players involved.

The serpent, the enemy, satan, the father of lies is always and will be crafty. His job is to twist and distort any and everything that is and make it look and sound a different way. The serpent will always cause you to second guess what you know you heard. He specializes in causing us to second guess and mess up the original plan and purpose for the instructions given. The serpent posed the question to the woman, "Did God really say you must not eat from any tree in the garden?" First of all, that is not what God said, God said, "You are free to eat from the trees in the garden, but you must not eat from the tree of the knowledge of good and evil for when you eat of it you will surely die." God gave this instruction to the man. and Adam relayed the message to the woman. They were free, without restriction to eat as much fruit from the vast variety of trees in the garden, just not this tree. All they had to do was stay away from those two trees, and everything would have remained consistent and stable.

> ***The woman said to the serpent, "We may eat fruit from the trees in the garden, but God did say, 'You must not eat fruit from the tree that is in the middle of the garden, and you must not touch it, or you will die.' " (Genesis 3:2-3)***

This one question, a twisted lie from the enemy made the woman who was later to be named Eve doubt in her mind the original instructions that were given. The interesting thing about Eve was she answered correctly when the serpent asked her the question. She was able to repeat verbatim the instructions from God and the consequences for not following the instructions, but why did she waver in what she knew to be right? Why did she want to touch what she could not have? I think maybe if she had walked away at that moment and not engaged in any more conversation with the enemy she may have passed the test and avoided going to the next level of sin. Sin starts as a thought, and if not stopped at that moment it will manifest into action if you think about it too long and engage in conversations in your mind with the enemy.

> *"You will not certainly die," the serpent said to the woman. "For God knows that when you eat from it your eyes will be opened, and you will be like God, knowing good and evil." (Genesis 3:4-5)*

The serpent came back at Eve with his rebuttal to her answer to his original question with a distorted version of the truth. The truth is, some things are true, but as parents, we protect children from the reality of that truth. In other words, it may be true, but you cannot handle the truth and the responsibility that comes with knowing the truth. The reality of the truth is what God was trying to prevent them from understanding is the fact they were not going to die physically, but they would die spiritually if they decided to eat the forbidden fruit. Yes, their eyes would be opened, and they would see things that God ordained to shelter them from seeing.

The questions of doubt and the birthing of disobedience comes when we know the truth, but we engage in conversations with the father of lies as he begins to make us question and contemplate, or maybe it will be okay this one time? Maybe God was not telling me the truth, and maybe the enemy really had inside information about the forbidden tree and fruit? God knows all and sees all way down the road, and he knows that once we think too long, then we will be tempted to touch and eventually indulge in that which is forbidden. It is for the reason God tells us to take every thought captive and make it obedient to Christ by shutting down any argument or conversation that does not line up with the word of God. Any conversations that set itself up against the knowledge of God.

The enemy set himself up above the knowledge of God by presenting Eve the inside scoop about the tree of knowledge of good and evil. The enemy knew that if he could lure her into questioning God and eventually disobeying God that she would forfeit a portion of her rights as a kingdom citizen. In actuality, she was setting herself up to become more like him and less like God by disobeying God and committing the first recorded sin.

> **When tempted, no one should say, "God is tempting me." For God cannot be tempted by evil, nor does he tempt anyone; but each person is tempted when they are dragged away by their own evil desire and enticed. Then, after desire has conceived, it gives birth**

to sin; and sin, when it is full-grown, gives birth to death. (James 1:13 – 15)

The woman believed the lie of the enemy and was enticed by his words and then she decided to yield to what she heard and after hearing and receiving Eve then looked at the fruit, and she liked what she saw and then eventually she touched what was forbidden to touch. The enemy's words tempted the woman, it was his words that aroused a desire in her mind, and once that desire was acted out, sin manifested. The sin when it was full-grown gave birth to death not an actual death but spiritual death and separation from God.

So people of God let us protect our ear gates by not engaging in any conversations that are not of God. These conversations can lead to desires that entice us to engage our eye gates to look upon and finally touch that which does not belong to us or can put us in harm's way. The consequence of the sin is not worth the bite.

CHAPTER EIGHT
"Eyes Wide Open"

Then the eyes of both of them were opened, and they realize they were naked; so they sewed fig leaves together and make covering for themselves. (Genesis 3:7)

When we sit down to eat dinner before we take the first bite, we eat with our eyes first. In addition to what we see, we smell the aroma of the food, and between the aroma and what we have seen; we are then encouraged to take a bite of food. I love to cook, and I was always told that presentation is essential to the meal experience. Poorly presented food sloppily placed on a plate is not inviting and could potentially be a turnoff.

The woman saw the fruit after the thought was placed in her mind by the enemy. The woman then acted on her desire by actually touching and then eating the fruit. She intentionally walked into disobedience to God because she chose to believe the lying whispers of the enemy. Also, because the enemy told her that she could obtain knowledge by eating the fruit, she desired to be like God because the enemy placed the thought in her mind. The enemy put the very idea in her mind that got him kicked out of heaven because he wanted to be like God. It is dangerous trying to be like someone else! Misery always enjoys company, and that is the enemy's plot and scheme, and that is to trick as many people as possible to join him in his defeated destiny. He wanted to be like God, and his perverted thinking that he could exalt himself above God caused him and some confused angels to get the left foot of fellowship on a one-way ticket to hell. The enemy's tactic is to confuse as many people as possible to follow him and set up his little kingdom; a kingdom that has no benefits only withdrawals. Eve's compromise with the devil immediately caused her to forfeit her God-ordained right as a kingdom citizen. She did not die, but without her knowing, she initiated a spiritual death and separation from God.

This ladies and gentlemen, sin that is, is what started the separation and disconnect of us walking in our God-ordained positions and callings in the kingdom. Sin is the act, but it is the thoughts that cause us to compromise and make unwise decisions. The thoughts as soon as the enemy introduces it in our mind must be cast down immediately and put to death. If the seed of the thought is left dormant, it can still germinate and cause rotten fruit to manifest.

How do we cast down the thoughts? Remove any and everything from your ear and eye gates that will remind you of that thought. If that means turning off the phone, the television, getting off of social media and last but not least deleting some people from your contact list. It may be necessary to change the company you keep if they are part of the negative influence. After you have removed the distractions, pray and ask God to replace those negative thoughts with God minded thoughts, His word.

> *Finally, brothers and sisters whatever is true, whatever is noble, whatever is right, whatever is pure, whatever is lovely, whatever is admirable; if anything is excellent or praiseworthy; think about such things. (Philippians 4:8)*

More importantly, pray and pray in the Holy Ghost and ask God to give you strength to resist the devil so he will flee from you! Replace the negative words with God's word and get off of Facebook and get in God's face and in His book! God had to remind me of this one day when the enemy tried to speak insecurities of my past that were birthed from the lies that were told to me as a child from well-meaning people. The enemy will attempt to speak to your weaknesses and make you think that he has a better solution by making you evaluate someone else's life and cause you to want to be like them to fulfill a void or empty place in your heart. The enemy will have you in a place of jealousy and strife because someone else's life in your social circle or your social media connections looks better than yours. Social media can sometimes place false expectations in your mind making you think that you are missing out on opportunities and can also create feelings of rejection because you feel you were left out of the social event of the century.

Only God's word and mercy can free you from such negative thoughts and perversions of the enemy. Only God can reveal the hidden intent of the seeds that have been planted in our hearts through deception by the enemy of our soul. We must cry out to God to fix our brokenness. We must also ask God to reveal the "you" that that is in Him; not the person that has evolved from the lies of the enemy. The person He intended us to be, His original design; His original DNA. There has to be a place of surrender to God where He can fix the broken me and take me to the end of me and replace that shattered person with the kingdom kid He ordained me to be from the beginning.

In our brokenness, we can be contagious. Just like a cold if we are not careful we can pass it on our hurt, pain, and insecurities to others by personal contact. The woman now convinced by the enemy to indulge passed on her desire to Adam through the power of influence. This power of influence from the enemy convinced the woman to look, see, touch and eventually take a bite of the forbidden fruit. It was also the power of influence that the woman used to give the fruit to her husband. In their minds what the enemy said was valid because they did not die after they ate the fruit they were still alive physically but the consequence of eating the fruit caused a spiritual death. How is it that after she ate the fruit, her eyes were not opened immediately? It was not until Adam ate and walked in disobedient agreement with the woman that both their eyes were opened at the same time. Is it possible, since God gave Adam the responsibility to govern the garden and teach the woman; I wonder if Adam chose not to eat the fruit if their spiritual eyes would have remained closed? The reality is they both had eyes, they could see everything in the garden, but maybe what God was trying to prevent them from seeing the reality of sin which is death, guilt, and condemnation.

When Adam ate the fruit, it sealed the deal, and because they believed the lie of the serpent their spiritual eyes opened and they both could see they were naked. The manifestation of sin pulls the covers back and exposes the naked vulnerability in our souls. During the pursuit of the sin all we see is what we want, but once sin is conceived and then birthed, it is after the fact that we look back and say, "What have I done?!" At that moment the enemy is standing back saying, "Gotcha!"

It is also at that moment your eyes open and you realize that you are naked and exposed. Then the guilt and condemnation rush into your heart, and because the weight of the disobedience is heavy, there is an overwhelming need to cover up what we have messed up.

Adam and the woman who was later to be named Eve had to come together and devise a plan to cover themselves. They had to piece together something to cover up their exposed bodies. Once sin is out in the open, then we try to piece together lies to cover up what we have done, thinking that the fragmented pieces will cover-up the lie. The pieces always fall apart, and the lie will be exposed because the truth will come bursting out because lies are only temporary fixes of fragile threads that cannot contain the truth.

Adam and the woman tried to find anything to cover themselves. They were very creative by piecing together the fig leaves to cover the most naked parts of their bodies, the private parts, but there were not enough fig leaves to cover up what happened that day in the garden. This is the same for us when we are trying to cover up our sin there will always be some skin exposed that reveals that something is terribly wrong with this picture.

CHAPTER NINE

"ADAM, WHERE ARE YOU?"

> *Then the man and his wife heard the sound of the Lord God as he was walking in the garden in the cool of the day, and they hid from the Lord God among the trees of the garden. But the Lord God called to the man, "Where are you?"(Genesis 3:8-9)*

Come out, come out, wherever you are! In the game of hide and seek this is the exclamation that is heard when it is okay to come out and stop hiding from the person that was declared, "it." The "it" person that had the responsibility of finding all of the hidden participants who had not managed to get past that person to the so-called safe place without being seen. Once the declaration is sounded, it is okay to come out of hiding and not be counted out of the game. The anticipation of the game was finding a place to hide and laughing and giggling because the person could not see you, but often you could see them as they searched for those in hiding. The added adrenaline rush was to sneak past them and make it to base safely before being caught.

Can you imagine how Adam and the woman felt as they were hiding from God for God to show up in the cool of the day and they could hear him walking in the garden, but they cannot see him? Wait a minute I thought their eyes were wide open now? So how is it that they could not see God with their new set of eyes? They were hidden, but they only heard the sound of His footsteps as God got closer to them. It appears they were playing hide and seek in reverse, but this time the "it" person is God, and he sees all and knows all and their very futile attempt to hide in the garden from the one who created the garden and everything in the garden was useless.

If Adam and the woman could not hide from God what makes us think that we can hide from God? Here we are in the middle of our sin in the cool of the day thinking we have gotten away with something in our little-tattered fig leaves which are barely covering up the nakedness of our sin. Then to add insult to injury, we try to hide in a deeper place thinking that God does not see us because we have managed to make a temporary covering. Often what we are trying to hide is apparent to the naked eyes of others around us. The bottom line is sin will cause us to make multiple layers in an attempt to cover up what is wrong, but it never fails what is done in the dark will come to light and be exposed in the cool of the day for all to see.

So here they are hiding and God already knowing what they did and where they were asked the man Adam, "Where are you?" Before God addressed Adam, the Bible says that they hid from the Lord God among the trees of the garden. The next word is pivotal to the scenario, "but the Lord God called to the man" says it all and that one word is "but." This one word "but" negates everything that is before this word in the sentence and grammatically speaking this one word says it all; they hid, but their hiding was in vain because at this point both of their butts were exposed and God was there to let them know that, and guess what, I see you, but you cannot see me.

When sin manifests we cannot see what we have done to ourselves and others. In other words, the sin blinds us temporarily until God steps in and exposes what we have done. The other word that stands out is God called to the man. God then addressed the man the "responsible one," the one that he had a covenant relationship with, and asked, "Where are you?" God asked the man because he gave Adam the directives and he was responsible. In the last chapter, it was not until man ate and fell into disobedience with God that his eyes and the woman's eyes were opened. When the sin manifested in the garden, the contract was broken; then everything started to fall apart. When God asked Adam, "Where are you?" He was asking him in the natural and in the spirit where are you? God was saying I see you trying to hide because of the sin you created and where are you in your spirit man now because of the sin?

That is the question we must ask ourselves when we knowingly take a bite of the fruit of sin and then ask ourselves was it worth it? In retrospect did the taste of what we know we should not ingest into our spirit worth God asking the question "where are you? Why have you forsaken your first love and why have you forsaken me for the bittersweet taste of the poison of sin?" When these questions and the realization of what we have done comes flooding into our spirit, and the weight of the remorse consumes our heart, the heaviness of the sin should break our hearts just like it breaks God's heart to see us blatantly disobey his word, his will and his way.

We have all faced this question at some point in our lives because the Bible says, for all have sinned and fallen short of the glory of God. It is the realization that sin does not please God and as his children, the disappointment of our actions hurt the heart of God. I know that we try to hide when that question is asked, and we also try to make up excuses to cover the action, but the bottom line is God is omnipresent and omnipotent. God is always present, so He sees all, and He is all-powerful, so He knows all things! So we might as well fess up and save ourselves some grief, and maybe He will be merciful in the punishment stage. Be encouraged to know the punishment and correction from God is necessary for spiritual growth and development. God is a loving father, so He chastens those He loves. The loving correction of God's hand will cause us to get back in step and in fellowship with Him.

CHAPTER TEN

"WHO TOLD YOU THAT YOU WERE NAKED?"

He answered I heard you in the garden, and I was afraid because I was naked, so I heated. And he said, who told you that you were naked? (Genesis 3:10-11)

When God asked Adam, "Where are you?" that was a two-fold question. God wanted Adam to answer Him with, where Adam was physically in the garden as well as where he was spiritually. Adam knew it was time to face God and he could no longer hide from the inevitable, and the inevitable was, Adam could no longer ignore the footsteps he heard earlier. Adam heard God coming before God asked him where he was hiding in the garden. Sin is just like that when we know that what we have done is about to catch up with us and call us out and expose what we thought we had so carefully hidden. Once the sound of the issue is face to face with us, we must admit, uh oh now it is time for me to answer and I can no longer pretend that the issue is staring me straight in the face. Once that moment comes the sound of our heartbeat, going; thump, thump, thump is now announcing that the reality of the truth is knocking at the door and we must answer.

Adam walked with God from the very beginning he was the first human being created, and now all of a sudden fear has crept into the camp. Adam was not fearful of anything because ignorance can surely be bliss. The unknown does not have to instill fear; often it is what has been revealed; that thing you can now see that stirs up fear and doubt. All of a sudden the knock of his heartbeat in his chest, a cadence larger than life consumed Adam, and he is now feeling something he never experienced before, and for the first time fear is overwhelming him and out of his mouth came the words, "I was afraid." Afraid of what? That is the question when the truth is knocking at the door of our hearts, "Saying let me in!" Adam was afraid because he was naked. All this time he did not know that he was naked, exposed, vulnerable and uncovered, but when sin steps in it snatches the covers off and exposes everything as we try to cover up all of our nakedness. So here is Adam exposed and naked, hiding in the trees with a few fig leaves trying to cover all of him and the woman that was with him. Adam's, attempt to cover themselves with fig leaves was like trying to use a handkerchief to cover up the most private parts of our bodies! Guess what? That is just not going to work! So when you hear someone coming and all you have is a handkerchief to cover yourself, the natural response is to

"Who Told you That You Were Naked?"

take cover, hide, run, and seek a place to make sure your naked body is not exposed and seen.

Their nakedness to God was nothing new. God wanted Adam to come face-to-face with him and say that he was naked and then God could ask the question, "Who told you that you were naked?" Who have you been talking to? What have you done to open your eyes to the fact that you were naked? Adam why are you hiding if you know that you have nothing to hide? God only asked Adam one question, but that one question is so deep and full of other questions. That is why when we mess up and operate out of the will of God layers of other questions evolve from our actions that eventually lead to the full-blown sin. The thought of the sin first, then we see with our eyes what we want, and then we meditate on what we want, we talk it over and over in our minds until we convince ourselves that is okay. Finally, the thoughts become action, and the sin is conceived and birthed, and now we are naked and saying, "What have I done?" It is at that moment that we come to ourselves and have to answer for what we have done.

Like it or not there is going to come a time that the question is asked and we must answer, "Who told you that you were naked?" Who lied to you and convinced you to exchange the truth with a lie? Who lied to you and told you things that are not true about you and caused you to step out of character out of who God created you to be? The truth is you have kingdom authority Adam, God gave you complete rule and reign over the entire garden and you mean to tell me because of one little piece of fruit you're getting ready to get you and your new bride kicked out, evicted from paradise! Yes, it is just that simple! One little piece of fruit caused Adam to forfeit the comfort and peace of the Garden of Eden. In the grand spectrum of things was that piece of fruit that good to lose everything? No! The lie the enemy tells us and sets us up for is; the bite of the fruit is worth the consequence.

When sin is birthed, we look at it, and it looks ugly! You mean to tell me I have forfeited my job, my family, my livelihood for this! What was I thinking! As you are lamenting and counting the cost, the enemy is in the background rolling on the ground laughing saying," I can't believe they fell for that!" The enemy is elated because he has accomplished his task of lying and convincing us that his way is better. It was also his job to plant seeds of doubt and fear so we can forget what God is telling us is the truth. Unfortunately, sometimes the lies of the enemy have come through others we trust. We believed what they have said about us, therefore missing our destiny by default and by no fault of our own, because we do not realize who we are and the true identity God gave us from the beginning.

So the question for those who did not do anything wrong but were wronged, "Who told you that you were naked?" At this point, this question is more of a rhetorical question of who lied to you? I hear God saying by the spirit," I am here now and I the Great I AM that I AM will show you the real you and erase all the lies that the enemy told you and cover you with the word and the truth!" The truth is I AM your covering, I AM your peace, and with me, you do not have to hide anymore. I AM here to cover you and protect you from the elements of life. I AM your father, and I will never leave you nor forsake you! Walk with me in the cool of the garden and let me show you the rivers of living water that flows freely here. You are a King's kid, and because you are my kid you are part of My kingdom, and you have rights as a kingdom citizen. So all the lies of the enemy are null and void, and I want you to walk in your kingdom clothes instead of the little fig leaves the enemy has offered you to cover up what he did to you. I am the tree of life, and the fruit from My tree is love, peace, joy, kindness patience. Today I offer all of this freely with no hidden agendas. My only agenda is to love you and help you to walk into your destiny.

CHAPTER ELEVEN

"THE BLAME GAME"

The man said, the woman you put here with me she gave me some fruit from the tree and I ate it. The Lord God said to the woman what is this that you have done? The woman said the serpent deceived me and I ate it. (Genesis 3:12–13)

There was a nursery rhyme game that I played as a little girl that went like this, "Who stole the cookie from the cookie jar?" I loved this game; we would sit in a circle singing the song asking the question who stole the cookie from the cookie jar? Then the first person's response was, who me? This phrase was followed by, "Yes you!" from the other participants and then the person who was accused would reply back, "Couldn't be!" Then the crowd would say, "Then who?" Then the first person's response was to point the finger to the next person in the line stating their name as the person that stole the cookie from the cookie jar. The objective of the game was never to resolve who took the cookies and always placed the blame on the next person for the stolen cookies.

The issue with this game just like the circle we were sitting in, the blame got passed around and around; never coming to any resolution because no one wanted to take responsibility for the stolen cookies. The fact is the missing cookies didn't start with just one cookie in the jar it began as a full jar of cookies, and each person had their hand in the cookie jar. After each person took a cookie from the cookie jar, no one wanted to admit they had any cookies or even played a part in the missing cookies. They would blame the next person as they all looked at each other with cookie crumbs on their hands and faces.

Well, this is a picture of the blame game that was about to take place in the garden that day when God walked into the area where Adam and the woman were attempting to hide the evidence of their sin. When God confronted Adam with his second question, He asked Adam was, "Have you eaten from the tree that I have commanded you not to eat from?" Unfortunately, Adam's response was not an answer to the question. God asked him, "Have you eaten from the forbidden tree? Adams correct response should have been a straightforward, "Yes," but his response was to the point blame towards the woman. Adam pointed to the woman by saying, "The woman," but he went a step further by, "Saying the woman you put here with me"; what!? So did Adam just try to in a very subtle way put God in the middle of this mess by saying

"The Blame Game"

God messed up because He put the woman there with him! Let the games begin, "Adam stole the cookie from the cookie jar! Who me? Yes, you! Couldn't be! Then who? The woman stole the cookie from the cookie jar!"

Adam, please wipe the crumbs off your face and dust your hands off before you start pointing fingers! Oh and by the way, is not a good idea to point your finger at God because you could not control yourself! So as Adam passed the baton to the woman, then God asked her, "What is this that you have done?" Again, the woman just like Adam did not answer the question directly but passed the blame; instead of saying, I messed up and ate the fruit, and after I ate it I suggested to Adam that it was good to eat. The woman's first words were, "The serpent," not that I messed up but, "The serpent deceived me, and I ate." The woman like Adam admitted in a round-about way that they ate but not before passing the blame away from themselves. So here we go again this time with the woman, "The woman stole the cookie from the cookie jar! Who me? Yes, you! Couldn't be! Then who? The serpent!"

The serpent, this is where this game started as the woman pointed her cookie crumbed finger to the one she listened to that started this whole issue that eventually led to the blame game. The serpent, the father of lies and deception, the accuser of the brethren our adversary. God's way is when two or three are gathered in my name I will be in the midst, but the enemy's way is where two or three are gathered together with me I will start mess, and that is precisely what he did then and continues to do now. After God addressed Adam and the woman about what they did He asked them questions so they could see where they were spiritually and not their physical location in the garden. God wanted to know where they were in their mindset. When they stepped into disobedience, they moved from a place of peace and tranquility into a place of condemnation and fear.

The enemy used the power of suggestion to convince the woman that it was okay to eat from the forbidden tree after the idea was planted in her thoughts the woman acted upon what she heard. The woman never had a conversation with the enemy she just listened to a one-sided discussion and agreed in her mind that it was okay to act upon what she knew was wrong. It is the power of suggestion that causes us to think and then act upon what we know to be wrong.

The power of suggestion is why it is imperative to guard our ear gates and our eye gates, so we are not tempted to reach out and touch and sample the bittersweet fruit of sin. I know we have all been tempted and have had our hand in the cookie jar at one point in our lives. We have all had the residue of sin all over us, but more importantly, than the residue is the fact that we can dust ourselves off and receive the healing cleansing power of Jesus that takes away all evidence of our sin.

CHAPTER TWELVE

"Consequences, Consequences, so God Said"

So the Lord God said to the serpent, "Because you have done this, "Cursed are you above all the livestock and all the animals! You will crawl on your belly and you will eat dust all the days of your life." (Genesis 3:14)

The power of suggestion is the lure that is used in many commercials that cause us to want to go out and buy that burger that has all the juices from the hamburger running down the arms of the person eating the burger. The purpose is to entice you to want to run to that burger joint to taste and see if it tastes as good as it looks. Often we think about that commercial and then make a final decision to make it happen. So you get in your car with the vision of burgers in your head and your mouth salivating ready to partake in what you have seen. Finally, you make it to the restaurant and place your order and now is just a matter of time what you have seen will be right before your eyes to taste and see. The anticipation of what you have envisioned is now getting ready to manifest right before your eyes. Wait for it! Wait for it! Finally, it is here, so you say, your grace, if you remember to say, your grace, then you take the first bite and then, all that anticipation comes to a screeching halt when you take the first bite. After you take the first bite, you find out to your dismay that it looked better than it tasted! All that for this great disappointment and let down! So you say to yourself was it worth it? The answer was no! I wasted gas, money and time for nothing and on top of it, this burger gave me indigestion! So the consequence of the power of suggestion from start to finish was a stomachache and money wasted!

When it comes to the incident in the garden that day it was the serpent that initiated the blame game by the power suggestion, but he did not directly eat of the tree he just suggested to the woman that the fruit is edible by telling her she would not die if she ate of the tree. The enemy's part was to plant the seed and to deceive her into believing him and not God. How is it that the one who suggests the crime or the mastermind walks away with somewhat clean hands and no visible evidence that directly links them to the incident? God questioned both Adam and the woman, and then he immediately addresses the serpent the mastermind with the power of influence and suggestion by saying to him, "Because you have done this." God already knew what they all did and their roles in the incident in the garden He just needed to let them all know, I see you, and I know what you did, and now you must all suffer the consequences for your blatant disobedience. In this case, the last person shall be first in their punishment. So God started with the serpent, the last person He addressed about the incident in the garden. God then began to administer the consequences for their actions.

> *So the Lord God said to the serpent, "Because you have done this, cursed are you above all livestock and all wild animals! You will crawl on your belly, and you will eat dust all the days of your life. (Genesis3:14)*

Got started with the serpent because He knew that the woman was not even thinking about the fruit from the tree. She was minding her own business when the enemy with his crafty self, walked into her presence and began to suggest that God did not know what He was talking about concerning the fruit from the tree of knowledge of good and evil. Then God addressed the evil one not with a question but a direct indictment of, "Because you have done this." God then announces, this is what I am going to do to you. He made it very clear because I am the Great I Am that I Am I have authority and power to change your structure, and since you decided to walk yourself into her space that day I am going to start off by taking away your legs. I AM going to make you uniquely different than any of the other animals in the garden. I am making you the lowest of low in the animal kingdom, and even if you did not want to eat dust, you have no choice but to eat dust as you move around on your belly. In addition, to that, I'm going to put an instant hatred and hostility between the woman and you because this suggestion has spiraled and downloaded into something bigger than just a bite of fruit. This one bite of fruit is going to cause physical pain for the woman because she listened and acted on your suggestion. Finally, in the end, the offspring of the woman will conquer and beat any seed or any offspring you try to birth. The final outcome in this game is your seed loses, and the seed of the woman will always win. In other words in the end, after the evil plot, we win! The "He" that God was speaking of is Jesus the one that was there from the beginning and the final outcome is the Word that was there from the beginning will crush the head of the serpent.

> *God then turned to the woman and said," I will make your pains in childbearing very severe with painful labor you will give birth to children. Your desire will be for your husband, and he will rule over you." (Genesis 3:16)*

Thanks a lot! Adam has not officially named you yet, but thanks a lot, Eve! For your part in causing all womankind to suffer in pain for something that could have possibly felt like a grape passing through the birth canal instead of a watermelon. For all the ladies out there, there are no words that can describe the level of pain and discomfort that was passed on to us from the first woman. For this, we say in unison and in concert and very sarcastically, "Thanks, Eve!"

Also, the original plan when God created man and then pulled the woman out of the man was they were created in his image. They were the same but different. God gave them the same authority to rule over the earth and subdue it and everything in the earth, but after her decision to listen to the now belly crawler the woman forfeited her original position to rule equally with Adam. Eve's desire is now for her husband and for him to rule over her.

The woman is still a kingdom citizen and has kingdom rights but if she is married her husband is to lead guide and direct her. Ladies this is why it is imperative that we hear from God to make sure the men we marry are men of God with God principles and ideas. We must be equally yoked with the man that God has ordained for our lives. So after God finished with the serpent and the woman, He declared the final consequences to Adam for his part in the garden incident.

> ***Then God said to Adam, "Because you have listened to your wife and ate the fruit from the tree about which I commanded you, "You must not eat from it, "Cursed is the ground because of you; through painful toil you will eat from it all the days of your life. (Genesis 3:17)***

Well, men, this is where the rubber meets the road, and now the consequences of Adam has affected you. The cost of Adam's disobedience was great. When God spoke to the woman, He did not say the word cursed, but for the serpent and Adam God use the word cursed. God cursed the serpent, but for Adam He cursed the ground that was given to him to watch over. The original plan for Adam was to work the garden and take care of the land and everything in the garden. God blessed Adam's assignment, and the blessings of God makes us rich and adds no sorrow to it! God placed them in the garden; the garden was a place of peace and serenity. Adam was the contract manager of the garden, and all he had to do was be who God created him to be and take care of the land. Adam's original job was not a job where he had to work hard or sweat he just needed to oversee the land and everything that was in the garden. In my imagination, the temperature must have been a constant comfortable temperature because after all Adam and the woman wore birthday suits. After God cursed the land everything changed for Adam because he did not fulfill the most important clause of the contract between himself and God, and that was to operate in complete obedience to God.

When a company falls, it does not matter who caused the breach if the CEO does nothing to stop the breach than the person who takes the biggest hit is the person at the top. God commanded Adam not to eat from the tree but because he was influenced by his wife and ate from the tree knowing he was disobeying God, that one bite caused him to lose his contract with God.

Men, it is important to obey God first and not be influenced by women, when God tells you to do something do what God tells you to do. This one act of disobedience has caused a spiral effect that continues to this day. The enemy influenced the woman, and the woman convinced the man to take a bite of what was forbidden.

There is nothing new under the sun this is still going on today! The downfall of many great men is the influence of a woman who is influenced by the father of all lies. I'm not speaking against women because I am a woman but do not be tricked into thinking what you see by the power of suggestion and influence is better than what God has ordained for you and ordained for you to do in His master plan. Adam's destiny was altered that day because of a simple act of disobedience. I am sure Adam may have reflected back thinking, it was not worth it to take one bite and lose my place of peace and comfort with God for a quick taste of forbidden fruit. This principle applies to both men and women our destinies are not worth forfeiting all that God has for us because the enemy has lured us into a trance and a moment of temporary insanity to do something that in the long run you will regret for the rest of your lives.

Not only did Adam lose the comfort of just chilling in the garden and not breaking a sweat, more importantly, God pronounced a death sentence on him that was not there previously. The plan was for the man and his wife to live happily ever after in the land flowing with every single provision they needed and their other assignment was to be fruitful and multiply. Now because of this one misstep Adam, the once immortal man stepped into mortality when God said, by the sweat of your brow you will toil for your food until you return to the ground. So God returned Adam at that moment to his original form because God breathed the breath of life into a clay man form from the dust of the earth. The provision of eternal life was now null and void in the garden.

Now the consequences of everyone that had their hand in or about the cookie jar has resulted in another game, ashes, ashes, we all fall down! When Adam fell, we all fell even though his wife took the first bite but in my holy imagination as I indicated in the previous chapter what would've happened if Adam did not eat and he corrected the woman for her disobedience? Is it possible that she and the serpent could have received their punishment and Adam would have retained His assignment in the Garden of Eden for all humanity? Oh well, this is not the end of the story, but it did undoubtedly change the original plan and tone that God had in mind.

Adam named his wife Eve because she would become the mother of all the living. The Lord made garments of skin for Adam and his wife and clothed them. (Genesis 3:20-21)

Usually, when a plan falls apart, there is a contingency plan that must be put in place to make provision for the breach or disconnect in the contract. The original idea was for Adam to name every creature, well when Adam was at work naming all

"Consequences, Consequences, So God Said"

the animals one animal the serpent was talking to the woman who had not yet been named. Adam's assignment was to name the woman, and if he had stayed focused on his task for the day the woman could have been named that day instead of Adam throwing away his original job for a fruit snack! So now that the plan of the enemy has been exposed and God has handed out the repercussions of the sin Adam is back on track and focused on one of his original assignment, including naming the woman. So for the first time, let's introduced to some and welcome to others, Eve! Her name, the woman's name is Eve. Adam named her Eve because she would become the mother of all the living beings. The other part of the contingency plan was for God to take off the tattered fig leaves Adam and Eve attempted to place on themselves in the greatest cover-up of all mankind. God had to fix what they messed up and make clothes of skins that would protect his creation from the elements. Even though they messed up, God still had a genuine love for them even though the Lord had to correct their behavior. Whom the Lord loves He chastens.

It is the same for us in all of our humanness God loves us but He hates the sin. He loves the man; his original creation. So when we mess up trust and believe there are consequences for our actions but on the same note, we have a loving father who will correct us and cover us when we mess up if we confess what we have done even if it is laced with cookie crumbs.

CHAPTER THIRTEEN

"THE FALL"

So the Lord God banished him from the garden of Eden to work the ground from which he had been taken. (Genesis 3:23)

After the fallout of a breach of contract, there must be a plan to make sure nothing like this ever happens again. So we see that God is having a conversation with the Trinity of himself Father, Son, and Holy Spirit about how to fix the problem in the garden. In my imagination I can hear the conversation going somewhat like this, Houston we have a problem! Security was breached, and if we do not take control we will lose complete control and guess what that is not about to happen! When God began the conversation about the problem in the garden, He was speaking specifically about one person, Adam, even though the enemy and Eve were involved, but God's conversation was about the man. Adam was God's original design His first human being the photo-type of himself. Adam was the one that God brought into covenant with Himself in the garden.

Adam was created to watch over God's creation, the land and everything in and about the land. Adam was responsible and held responsible for the fall of humanity. This breach of the contract not only affected Adam and Eve but affected all of humanity down the line. The original plan was for us all to live the blessed life in the garden with no worries or cares of life. The problem was when Adam ate of the fruit he stepped into a realm that was not intended for him to step into and that was knowing the difference between good and evil. Before he ate the fruit of the tree although he named the serpent, he did not know that the serpent had evil motives against God. The serpent's motive that day was to abort the plan of God because he was banned from heaven because of his high attitude about himself thinking he was going to exalt himself above God. The serpent did not approach Adam that day in the garden it is very possible things may have gone in a different direction if he had, but he approached Eve. He walked over to Eve and started talking to her. Wait a minute you mean animals can talk in the garden! That revelation just hit me that the serpent actually spoke to the woman. Okay, I'm back. The serpent spoke to Eve Adam's rib, bone of his bone about a minor but significant change in the original contract. All changes or amendments to a contract must be filtered through the contract manager, and the contract manager was Adam, not Eve.

This is how the enemy gets in he studies the particulars of our destiny, and he will use any means necessary to cause a breach of contract even if he has to use someone else to get to you. He does not come direct he always comes through the side door, backdoor, sneaking in any way he can to cause a break, a little hole that will eventually rip everything apart. So while Adam and Eve were probably sitting back thinking about what they had done the conversation was happening in God's boardroom on how to secure the Tree of Life. I can only imagine how they were feeling, just like little children knowing they were in big trouble, sitting down real quiet reflecting on how they could have done things differently. We have all been there at some point in our lives when we have to sit back and wonder, "Okay I know the first round of punishment has come, but there has to be more because this was a big problem and we are in big trouble."

> **So the Lord God banished him from the Garden of Eden to work the ground from which he had been taken. (Genesis 3:23)**

God, because He is God could have made Adam and his wife go bye-bye, but because God loved His creation God decided to remove them from the garden and not just wipe them off the face of the earth. He could have started over and created a different photo type, but He had mercy on them both and put them out to work the land that He used to make Adam. God's mercy and compassion is amazing because things really could have been different that day because of what Adam and Eve did, but God!

What happened that day in the garden was a BIG problem, but we serve a BIG God, and His heart is as big and as wide and as deep as an ocean, and it is full of love! It was the love and grace of God that allowed Adam and Eve to continue to live in the land of the living. It is the same love that God used that day, it was tough love, but it was still love. God loved Adam enough to save himself from himself.

So after a plan falls apart and then you begin to think maybe I should have done this myself? Well, that is what happened God had to regroup and come up with another plan for humanity since the first plan failed the test. As bad as things went that day in the garden God's contingency plan is even better, because a new revised Adam was on the way. No worries about getting to the tree of life because the new Adam is the tree of life!

CHAPTER FOURTEEN

"And the Last Shall be First, The Second Adam"

So it is written the first man Adam became a living being but the last Adam, a life-giving spirit. (I Corinthians 15:45)

When it comes to life and life experiences the second time around can sometimes be a better experience because the first time was a time of testing and trial. The first try can give you the opportunity to learn and grow from your mistakes. I remember the first time I made a cake from scratch I forgot to put in the baking powder a small but significant component that is required to cause the cake to rise. Well needless to say the cake was very dense, and it was flat as a pancake. After that epic fail, I was somewhat hesitant to attempt to bake another cake, out of fear of messing up again. I was a novice at baking, and I did not understand what happened but when I discussed the situation with my home economics teacher she was able to explain why the cake did not rise. So I tried again and the next time I made sure I did not miss the baking powder and the cake turned out the way that I had envisioned.

Well, when God created the first man Adam in his image and likeness He created him from the dust of the ground and then breathed life into this clay vessel, and it became a living being, a human being. God declared that the creation was good and it was good because God declared him to be so. The plan was good, and Adam was in agreement with God concerning his earthly assignment until he got off track. Why is it that he got off track? He was made in God's image, right? So what ingredient was missing? I would like to suggest that maybe the main ingredient Adam was missing was the character of God? The definition of character according to Webster is, "The mental and moral qualities distinctive to an individual." Some of God's character traits are He is good; He is kind, He is compassionate, He is love, He is just and because He created everything there was and is to be created; He is a man that cannot lie. These are just a few of the character traits that describe God, some of the qualities that describe the mind and the moral compass of God. One significant characteristic that describes God is that He cannot lie. Whatever He says is the final word, and there is no negotiation. When God told Adam not to eat from the tree, and the consequences of death, He meant that. God knew that Adam would not die physically, but he would die spiritually because he did not follow the instructions given.

It was a lie that caused the problem, the issue in the garden that day. It was the mindset that I am going to do what I want to do regardless of what the contractual agreement between God and Adam. Adam's realization after the fact is what caused him to go in deeper to try to attempt to fix what he made wrong that day. Can you imagine the disappointment that God felt knowing that His creation that was in His image was now acting out of character of what He had envisioned in His original plan? I'm sure it broke His heart to see Adam take a bite of the fruit particularly since the original covenant was between Adam and God. Yes, of course, God saw the enemy as he approached Eve in the garden and he saw her take that first bite, knowing that she had slipped into disagreement with God first and her husband second. I'm just wondering if God was thinking well maybe, just maybe Adam the first human being that I created would do what is right and not yield to the temptation of sinning by going against God by doing what He told him not to do. Again, in my imagination, I can envision God sitting back saying, "Don't do it, don't do it!" "And then, awww! He did it! He took a bite!"

It is the same hurt and disappointment that is felt as a parent when you tell your children not to do something, and you find out they did the exact opposite. The first time this happens, and you know your children know better it is very painful. It hurts to know children decided to do it their way and painful for them to find out that their way was very wrong. The part that hurts more is the fact that you must punish them so they learn from their mistake of doing it their way. The punishment is a part of the process, and this step must not be overlooked otherwise the child will not fully grow into the man or woman of God that He has ordained for them to be before the foundations of the earth.

God created Adam to be a living being but because he did not possess the full character of God it wasn't possible for him to maintain the Commandments of God without the Spirit of God dwelling in him. Is it possible that Adam could have continued his job in the garden? I must say no because without the presence of God moving within him and instructing him he could not control his mind, will, and emotions. It was his mind that was compromised first by thoughts and after his mind was compromised the enemy was able to creep in and cause him to think about taking a bite of the fruit. Once the seed of sin is planted the battle of the will goes on, if only for a moment, "Should I do it or should I not do it; that is the question?" Once the decision has been made, and we have settled it in our will to act upon the thought then sin is birthed and manifested. After the sin has manifested, the enemy is laughing at us, and the emotional roller coaster of guilt and condemnation starts and there is no off button to shut it down. Thank you, God! Thank you, Father! You are the off button, and you can make it stop because you had the perfect contingency plan to replace the first Adam in the person of Jesus the Christ!

In the beginning was the Word and the Word was with God and the Word was God. He was with God in the beginning. Through him

all things were made, without him, nothing was made that has been made. In him was life and that life was the light of all mankind. (John 1:1)

After the fall God had to send His son who was and is to come to the earth to fix what the first Adam messed up. God had to send the word that was used in the beginning to create everything in the earth to correct the security breach in the garden. Jesus, the word of God, was a part of the conversation from the beginning when God said, "Let us create man in our image" and He was a part of the conversation when God put Adam in the garden. So what better replacement to save humanity than the word wrapped in flesh, Christ Jesus. God had to wrap his Spirit, the same spirit that hovered over nothing to create a replacement to redeem man back to God. His son was sent to accomplish what the first Adam could not do, and that was to maintain a relationship with God. Jesus had to come to fix the broken relationship between God and humanity. Jesus came to speak life and restore life so man could have a relationship with God. Jesus is that life giving spirit that redeems the time we have all lost from the mistakes of our past. Things we have said and done that have separated us from God and his original plan for our lives. Jesus also came to correct the lies that were told to us by no fault of our own by others that were used by the serpent to derail us from our Godly assignments. Lies that were whispered in our ears as children that caused us to wander off to find covering and shelter. The lies about us that made us walk into areas God never intended for us to walk. Jesus is here to ask the question, "Who told you that you were naked? Who lied to you and told you that you were not a King's kid and caused you to forfeit your God-ordained kingship?" Jesus, the second Adam, came to speak life and let us know that after He left the earth realm that the Holy Spirit was coming to dwell within us and show us the character of God so that we could have life through Jesus Christ. He came so that we could love, live and forgive as He does on a continuous basis. Without the love of Jesus and the power of the Holy Spirit, this is the only way we can love, live and forgive the way our father loves and forgives us even when He has to chasten us for broken fellowship as a result of sin.

Jesus the tree of life, the second Adam came so we can have everlasting life, the life that was intended for us from the beginning. I thank God for Jesus the tree of life that reached down one day and saved me from myself as I was attempting to hide behind my fig leaves of sin. I will never forget the day that I felt the tangible presence of God as He held me and comforted me after I had done all I thought that I was big and bad enough to get away with. The day when I was at the end of me, and I had nowhere else to turn, tired of running, tired of hiding in the forest of trees called life and life experiences. I remember the day He asked me, "Who told you that you were naked? Who lied to you and told you that you would never amount to anything because you did not look the way that you should look and "No one will want you if you are fat and funny looking?" The same one that said, "That if it is not the right the first time it was wrong," leaving no room to learn from my experience. The lies that planted seeds of perfectionism and rejection. Thank you God for fixing my scared and messed up heart and giving me a new life through your darling son Jesus the Christ! My big brother, my Redeemer, my friend, my Lord and my Savior hallelujah!

Thank you, Jesus for giving me a second, third, fourth, and too many chances to number at life. Thank you, God, for giving me a second chance and not letting me perish because I messed up just like Adam and Eve did in the garden. Even in that, you made provision for me to still be in the land of the living and that you provided a way back to you through your son Jesus the second and the last Adam. All the Adam I need to live and breathe and have my being! All I can say is thank you God for not giving up on me and giving me an opportunity to be a part of your beautiful masterpiece that you have for my life. Thank you, God, for creating me with a desire to love and worship You, and with the free will to obey You through the power and the presence of the Holy Spirit through Jesus Christ.

Now as I finish penning the end of this book that God allowed me to write. I ask by the power the Holy Spirit this question, "Who told you that you were naked?" And after you answer the question if you are not saved, and you do not know Jesus ask Him to come into your heart. Ask Jesus to cover you and remove the fig leaves of life that you have put on to cover the sin and imperfections that have wounded your soul. Let Jesus breathe the breath of life into your spirit so that you can breathe and live again. If you do not know Jesus as your Lord and Savior, please pray this prayer. "Lord Jesus, come into my heart. Lord I know I have sinned, and I need you to cover me and save me with your love, the same love that you demonstrated when you died on the cross by shedding your blood on Calvary. I repent of my sins and I am asking you to forgive me for those sins. I acknowledge you as the Son of God the second Adam that came to redeem me back to God. Thank you, Jesus!" Receive him in your heart and say amen! It is just that simple.

If you have prayed this prayer, you are saved, and now you have the privilege of living the blessed life because you are now connected to God through the Tree of Life Jesus! Glory hallelujah! Now use the last few pages of this book to pour out of your spirit a love letter to God thanking Him for saving you through the blood and the power of His Son Jesus the Christ! Thank you God! Thank you, Jesus! Amen! It is finished!

Write a Love Letter to God

CPSIA information can be obtained
at www.ICGtesting.com
Printed in the USA
LVHW011644070720
659997LV00011B/1106